A PHŒNIX TRANSFORMED

by
MARGARET LEWIS

All proceeds from the sale
of this book go to the
Royal Liverpool Philharmonic Society
to further its important work in the community

First published 1995 by Countyvise Limited, 1 & 3 Grove Road, Rock Ferry, Birkenhead, Wirral, Merseyside L42 3XS.

Copyright © 1995

ISBN 0-907768-81-4

All rights reserved. No part of this publication may be reproduced, stored in a retrieval system, or transmitted, in any form, or by any means, electronic, chemical, mechanical, photocopying, recording or otherwise, without the prior permission of the publisher.

Contents

Foreword	Sir Desmond Pitcher (Chairman of Merseyside Development Corporation and Royal Liverpool Philharmonic Society Trust)	i
Acknowledgements		iii
Introduction		iv
I	Overture: The Hall on the Hill	1
II	A Phœnix out of Ashes	8
III	Home of a 'Royal' Musical Centre	14
IV	Interlude: A Symphony of Friendship	18
V	A First-Class Home for a World-Class Orchestra	26
VI	Coda: Into the Future with the Hall's Ambassadors from Liverpool	34
Some Useful Information		39
List of Royal Liverpool Philharmonic Orchestra Principal Conductors		43
Chorusmasters of the Royal Liverpool Philharmonic Choir		48
The Merseyside Youth Orchestra		51
List of Photographs		53
References		55

Foreword

I was thrilled when Margaret Lewis asked me to write the foreword to her delightful chronicle of the Philharmonic Hall. There is no doubting the passion and pride she feels for our Great City of Liverpool. It is a beautifully written labour of love.

Liverpool is steeped in history and pride. It played a full part in the building of the British Empire as a leading port and trading centre and for some two centuries was a gateway to the New World.

Today, Liverpool is famous the world over for its cultural and sporting ambassadors. From its football clubs and the Beatles to our own celebrated orchestra and choir, The Royal Liverpool Philharmonic, which continues to play such an important role in bringing international recognition to our City.

First opened in 1849, the Philharmonic Hall was tragically destroyed by fire in 1933. Rebuilding took place before the war, at the end of which the Hall emerged unscathed by the bombings. This autumn sees the opening of the refurbished Philharmonic Hall, one of Liverpool's most majestic and important buildings and a fitting home to one of the oldest concert orchestras in Europe.

Miss Lewis' charming anthology reflects lovingly on the history of the Hall and its immense contribution to Liverpool life. It is full both of wonderful anecdotes, such as the one of the white lady who haunts the Hall, and also of reflections on the colourful personalities, notably Sir Charles Groves, who have dominated the Hall and the orchestra. Since its first trip to the European mainland in 1966, the orchestra has been in great demand on the international touring scene and this book is a lasting tribute to everyone involved with the Hall and its music.

I'm sure you will enjoy reading 'A Phœnix Transformed' as much as I have and that you will continue to enjoy the music made in the Philharmonic Hall for many years to come.

Sir Desmond Pitcher DL

September 1995

This booklet is dedicated to Walter Runacus
who gave forty-three years of devoted service
and loyalty as a member of the 'Phil's' staff

Acknowledgements

In one sense this booklet is like a mosaic. A picture is built up from pieces of information culled from a variety of sources. The writer is simply an editor who, through selection of appropriate material and personal observation, has attempted to present an overall picture from the fascinating pieces of knowledge acquired over the years. All credit and gratitude goes to the following institutions and people upon whose work the 'picture' has been built.

I wish to thank the Royal Liverpool Philharmonic Society for permission to use biographical details and selected photographs.

My thanks are due, also, to the publishers of the Liverpool 'Daily Post' for allowing publication of photographs and extracts from articles.

Many individuals have helped in a variety of ways and given their time so generously. In particular, I am grateful to Lady Groves for her interest in the booklet's production and for her help in providing information about Sir Charles's years in Liverpool. To Sir Desmond Pitcher, one of the busiest people in the country, I am indebted for his making time to write the Foreword.

To those whose daily lives are connected directly or indirectly with the Society I wish to mention the following - the Chief Executive, Mr. Antony Lewis-Crosby who has been unstinting in his help, generous in giving his time, and always understanding; the Society's Archivist, Mr. V C Tyndall and Mrs Tyndall for their encouragement, wise advice and appreciated service of proof-reading; Mr. Geoffrey Cowie for his enthusiastic discussion about M.Y.O. programmes and past events connected with the Youth Orchestra; Mr. Stuart Christie for his valued information about past chorusmasters; Mrs Eleanor Wright for allowing the use of her article about the Choir; Miss Sandra Parr for reading the script and providing interesting background information particularly about the MYO; Mr. Ian Archer for his great help with photographs, and his cheerfulness when so frequently interrupted by my questions, and Mr. Andrew Bentley, who very smartly provided all the information I needed about the refurbished Hall.

Though not connected with the Society except through membership of Brock Carmichael Associates, the architects responsible for the Hall's refurbishment, Mr. Stuart Miles has been helpful in providing artists' impressions of the building. I thank him for his interest and time spared during such a busy schedule.

Similarly, I am indebted to Mr. Mark Proctor of Printfine for his generous giving of time, creative ability, interest and good humour; to Mr. and Mrs Emmerson of Countyvise Limited for assistance and advice over matters of publication, and to Mr. Rob Evans for loyal support and assistance over the business of distribution.

Introduction

"That Hall is no use to the likes of us - it is only fit for the posh folk. You see them there rolling up in their cars and coaches. The building should be pulled down and the money used for its upkeep given to the unemployed of the city".

The first sentence of this contemporary Liverpudlian's comment certainly contained some truth between 1849 and the beginning of World War II. However, the social changes in Britain, particularly in the last thirty years, have been such that concert audiences are now composed of people from every type of social background, with music enjoyed by all and not just the favoured few. How has this welcome change come about and why was the Hall built in the first place? An attempt has been made to suggest answers to these questions but I felt compelled to write this booklet for two other reasons.

There is a large section of Merseyside people who have a vague notion of 'what goes on' in the Philharmonic Hall yet have never been inside, or, perhaps feel that they wouldn't hear 'their sort of music' in such an 'élitist' establishment. It is hoped that these Merseysiders are encouraged to go and see the refurbished Hall following its re-opening in the Autumn of 1995 and find something of interest in the wide range of events. There is much more taking place than concerts of classical music.

The second reason is due to my love of, and pride in, Liverpool. It saddens me to see so much lethargy and indifference. It would appear that Liverpool rarely does justice to itself. It takes outsiders to see the fine spirit of true Liverpudlians, the magnificence of architecture and beauty of design of our city. Of course there are eye-sores, ugliness, litter and problems, but this is true of most cities in the present social climate.

There is no doubt that Liverpool is gradually overcoming her period of decline and re-emerging to become the fine city she once was. Her new 'image' will be different from that of the past and I am proud to be able to take part in this resurgence.

Many factors, institutions and individuals are contributing to this re-awakening and the booklet tells of one of them - the Royal Liverpool Philharmonic Society, which, through 'the goings on' at the Hall, has an Orchestra, Choir and Youth Orchestra bringing international recognition to the city.

The booklet is not a history but attempts, through key facts and anecdotes, to link the events in the Philharmonic Hall with Liverpool and Merseyside and to show what has been done for the area over the years through devoted hard work and interest.

Though written primarily for those people unaware of the importance of the Hall to Liverpool and surrounding areas, it is hoped that some of the Hall's 'regular' patrons will enjoy it also.

This interesting photograph from an old print must not be taken as an exact likeness. The artist has added chimneys and some embellishments.

i
Overture • The Hall on the Hill

It is now impossible to discover just what circumstances led to the formation in 1840 of the Liverpool Philharmonic Society which can claim to be the fifth oldest surviving concert-giving organisation in Europe. The older Festival Choral Society was still flourishing with an hundred-strong Chorus and sizeable Orchestra of a mixture of amateurs and professionals. Possibly, enlightened musical opinion in the town (as it then was) found the singing or the playing - or even both - inadequate. Whatever the reasons for its foundation, the new Society maintained amicable relations with its predecessor, and both had plenty of performing members in common right up to the closure of the older Society in 1860.

The Liverpool Philharmonic Society (not 'Royal' until 1957) began modestly enough in 'Mr. Lassell's Saloon', a dancing academy in Great Richmond Street. There was an Orchestra and Chorus of fifty. The Orchestra like the Festival Choral Society, consisted of both amateur and professional players and was, in 1841, of sufficient proportions to perform Beethoven's Symphony in C minor. In 1845, Mr. Lassell's Saloon was replaced by a foundry, and the scene of the concerts changed to the hall of the Liverpool College, later the Collegiate Institution in Shaw Street. It was during this time that greater plans were being made to ensure the longevity and success of the Society, its Orchestra and Choir.

The committee drew up a contract to buy a piece of land in Hope Street from the Mayor and aldermen of Liverpool '... whereon to erect and build a Concert Hall with boxes and stalls and open seats and with necessary and appropriate rooms and appendages'. John Cunningham was the chosen architect and in 1846 the foundation stone for the first Liverpool Philharmonic Hall dedicated to '... the science and practice of Music and other scientific and literary purposes connected with such science and practice was laid'.

Obviously, the Society did not believe in half measures, for it is recorded that in 1849 when the Hall opened, the Orchestra had grown to a total of ninety-six players, nearly all professional, and many imported from London. Of the ninety-six players there were twenty first violins, eighteen seconds, fourteen violas, twelve 'cellos and twelve double basses.

It was with this large Orchestra that six separate concerts, three of them 'grand miscellaneous' ones, marked the opening of the new Hall on 27th August 1849. The celebration of its opening had been 'a topic of general interest among the musical circles of Lancashire and the surrounding counties for nearly two years ...'. so commented a 'Times' correspondent some of whom were present and their remarks give a vivid picture of what the Hall and audiences were like. Some of these reports are as follows.

The building cost £30,000 'which though a high figure, was nothing extraordinary for such a rich commercial town as Liverpool, and was speedily raised'.

The opening concert was to have had a setting of Milton's 'Comus', commissioned by Mendelssohn and directed by him had he not died in 1847. The concert was not very well attended for two reasons. First, rumours had rapidly spread that the roof might collapse because no columns could be seen supporting it, and secondly, the price for a seat not occupied by subscribers was one guinea - a large sum of money at this time. As nobody was hurt and no roof collapse took place, the following concerts were well attended. With regard to the high price for seats the correspondent of 'The Times' of Thursday, 30th August 1849, wrote, 'The Liverpool public complain bitterly of the exclusive system adopted by the Committee of the Philharmonic Society ...'. The Society, in an effort to be exclusive and reward those members who had purchased boxes, stalls seats or shares in the Hall for their families in perpetuity, had set 'an extremely high entrance price of one guinea, and thereby ensured that more than half the Hall was empty'. This report substantiates the remark made in the Introduction to this booklet. The 'exclusiveness' was to continue until well after the end of World War II.

Fortunately, 'The Times' reporter was heeded by the Society and for the remaining celebratory concerts the price of seats for the general public was reduced so that the attendance at the final grand miscellaneous concert 'was brilliant and numerous'. However, criticism of the length of concerts which often lasted for four hours, referred to 'its inordinate length ... midnight had long passed before the last overture was over'. A heartfelt comment upon similar lines came from the correspondent reporting on Friday's concert - 'Another concert of four hours and a quarter duration! When will the directors of musical festivals take into consideration the wholesome adage "Enough is as good as a feast"?'.

The appearance of the interior of the Hall was quite magnificent especially as the new electricity was used. 'The hall is lighted in daytime by four large windows, two on either side'. The appearance of the Hall when lit at night 'is exceedingly brilliant, and fully satisfied the anticipations of everyone'. The lighting 'produces an effect absolutely fairy-like'.

The same 'Times' correspondent reporting upon Friday's long concert paid tribute to the ladies of Liverpool. 'The "Lancashire witches" as the ladies of this part of the world are familiarly designated, besides their personal attractions which are proverbial, are thoroughly versed in the secrets of the toilette and a more beautiful and enlivening spectacle than

The Philharmonic Hall and New Chapel

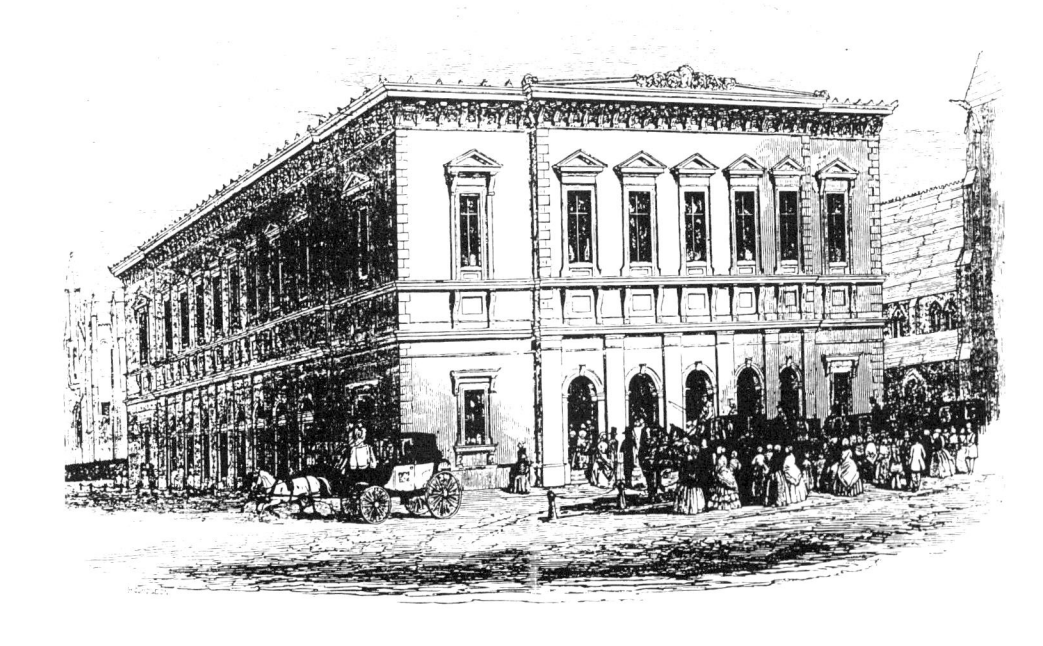

Exterior of New Philharmonic Hall at Liverpool

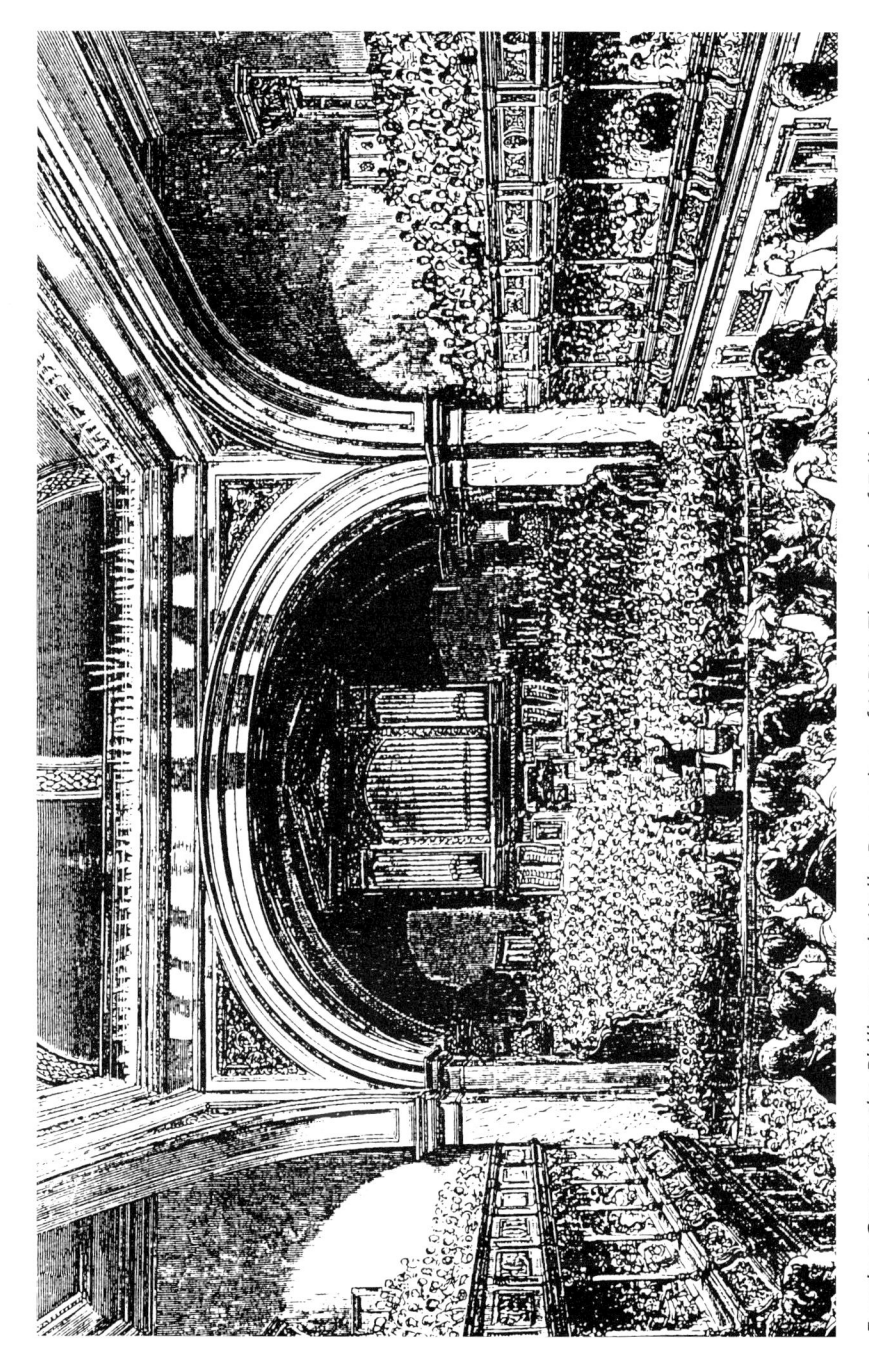

Evening Concert at the Philharmonic Hall - Reception of H.R.H. The Duke of Edinburgh

that presented by the vast area of the Philharmonic Concert Hall last night might be looked for in vain'. The Society's committee must have felt very satisfied with the week's celebration and with most of the reports from 'The Times'.

The appearance of the Hall, the beauty of the ladies, the brightness of the new electric light - all these visual elements seemed to appeal to newspaper reporters and journalists of the Victorian era. They were especially interested in a foreigners' ball, which was an annual event held at the Philharmonic Hall, and the 'Liverpool Review' of 12th January 1889, describes the eighteenth such event. 'The orchestra was again most beautifully and elaborately arranged as an Italian garden scene. Palms, blooming azaleas, hypathicas and tree ferns mingled together in cool refreshing, shady luxuriance - some of the plants reaching the stalwart height of nine feet'. The foreigners' ball was the chief event of a public character during the season and obviously there was space for dancing.

The 'Liverpool Review' reporter refers to this when he gives us a glimpse of the happy scene - 'The top galleries are ... quite bare. The gorgeous private boxes round the hall have each their occupants, who prefer the pleasure of looking on to that of dancing,' but '... downstairs among the throng ...not exactly to mingle, for at every step one is in danger of damaging a lady's train.' It is clear from the journalistic reports of the day that all the orchestral events of every nature were carefully planned and organised.

It is impossible to mention the names of all those concerned with the early organisation of the Society, but one can hardly omit the name of William Sudlow who became the first secretary. William played the organ for the Society until 1846 and after fifteen years as secretary he mysteriously disappeared, an event which caused considerable stir in Liverpool. He was suspected of having stolen an amount of the Society's funds though this was never proved.

Despite problems of all types, including the First World War, but particularly financial, the Society continued for eighty-four years giving excellent musical concerts in the Hall described by Hans Richter as 'the finest in Europe'. Yet, one of the Annual Reports revealed that 'owing to the non-payment of Subscriptions by a large number of Proprietors until late in the year ... some loss of Interest is occasioned'. Consequently, defaulters were fined for non-payment. Certain basic human characteristics remain the same through the centuries!

Unfortunately, as late as 1909 programmes show evidence of rigid social divisions, carrying curt reminders that only army and naval officers, ministers of religion and members of Proprietors' families could be admitted to their boxes. If a Proprietor wished to sell his seat only a person of whom the Society's committee approved could become his successor.

From the outset a marked atmosphere of what we should regard today as social snobbery dominated the Society's rules of membership.

Subscriptions were only accepted from 'persons of proved respectability'. This determination to exclude the under-privileged and the working-classes, save for admission to specially segregated cheap seats, only began to disappear - officially at least - in 1939. A relic of this attitude was still discernible for a few years after, when hard core 'old-timers' resisted every appeal of the management to attend any concerts other than the fortnightly Tuesday Subscription Series. For something like a century there was a decided social 'one-upmanship' about being a Phil subscriber, and generations of worthy people must have endured agonies of boredom simply because it was 'the thing' in Liverpool's higher circles to be known as a regular tenant of a box or stall. Part II of this booklet will reveal how completely this snobbish attitude has changed today.

The first Hall held two thousand, one hundred people, plus two hundred and fifty Orchestra and Chorus seats. Though situated somewhat outside the main busy thoroughfares of Liverpool and on a hill, its position in the newly developed area of Hope Street at its junction with Myrtle Street, was good. The wealthy property owners of Rodney Street and Abercromby Square were within walking distance, though carriages would be used. In fact, the early programmes carried references to the times when carriages should arrive at the end of concerts and all horses' heads had to face the same way, in the Myrtle Street direction. Adjacent to the Hall was New Chapel which catered for the spiritual needs of a flourishing population living in the area of the Hall.

Concerts were well-attended by the gentry and professional classes, and right from the start the Society upheld the tradition of bringing the finest musicians and singers to Liverpool as guest performers in the Hall. The same applies today, but during the Hall's earlier years conditions for patrons of concerts were very different. Only the two upper side galleries were open to the general public and free from the obligatory full evening dress for all Subscription Concerts. The auditorium was brightly illuminated throughout the evening. There was no dimming of lights and it was easy to follow a score. There was no bar, and the perambulating patrons during the lengthy interval presented an impressive picture of Liverpool 'society'. Many people went to the Philharmonic (never 'Phil' in those days) as much to be seen by others as to enjoy the music. In the early years of the Hall's existence a doorman, resplendent in gold-braided frock-coat and cockaded topper, announced in stentorian tones the arrival of 'Sir William So and So's carriage' or, as time went on - 'Mr. Whosit's motor'. The clatter of horses' hooves and the ring of harnesses gave way over the years to the mechanical background sounds of an occasional Daimler, Benz or Lanchester accompanied by the metallic shutting of doors.

There are still people today who remember the first Hall with its vast coved and coffered ceiling-span upheld only by the superbly swinging side and end arches unbroken by any pillar. The platform was spacious and had tiered chorus seats dominated by an impressive, but not beautiful organ case. The décor was cream and gold contrasting with the warm red upholstery of stalls and box seats which were certainly not comfortable. Even so, the concerts continued with regularity until, unexpectedly, disaster struck.

On the night of 5th July 1933 wisps of smoke were spotted coming from the roof of Cunningham's Hall and by morning it was a charred ruin. It was a spectacular fire and almost everything was lost, including two grand pianos and the new organ installed only three years previously. However, parts of the railings still exist - one as a door stop -and this was used when the Friends of the Phil chose their logo in 1982.

The great Hall no longer existed yet, in one sense, the fire of 1933 solved a serious problem for the Society. The stranglehold exerted by the box proprietors' freehold would have made reform difficult. The fire caused all freeholds to go for ever and though the new design of the second Hall faithfully restored the boxes, their seats have always been freely bookable like all the others.

Two links with the original Hall - remains of the damaged plaque (left) and Clara Butt, representative of the many great artistes who perfromed in the Hall.

ii
A Phœnix out of Ashes

A.K. Holland, a well-known music critic and prolific programme-note contributor for the Society, was an eye-witness of the 1933 fire. He remembered standing amid the ruins on Thursday morning, 6th July 1933 and feeling a sense of dismay. 'It was, I think, generally felt that the city had lost an artistic treasure. The salvage was of sentimental interest - portraits of famous musicians, some musical scores of permanent value, and an impregnable safe which contained one or two items of curiosity - these were retrieved.' However, 'the masterpiece of John Cunningham the architect, and all 'that it meant in the social and cultural amenities of the city, seemed to have passed away'.

The misfortune was all the greater in that the Society was looking forward to the prospect of celebrating the centenary of its existence, but there was never any real doubt that the Hall would be re-built. The insurance money from the disastrous fire was to be used and added to the funds which were soon raised. Herbert Rowse, the Liverpool architect of the Mersey Tunnel and Martin's Bank Building in the city's commercial centre, was commissioned to design a new Hall.

Apart from announcing the venue for concerts as being the Central Hall, Renshaw Street, there is nothing in the 1933-34 programmes to inform today's reader that anything was amiss - even in the face of unparalleled disaster the Philharmonic Society maintained its traditional composure. During the interim, concerts proceeded much as before, except that programmes demanding full Choir and Orchestra were transferred to St. George's Hall. Despite loss of revenue and membership, the Society weathered the storm and by 1938 it was confidently hoped that the new building would be ready by the following January. There were the usual last-minute delays and it was not until the 19th June 1939 that the second Hall was formally opened by Sir Hugh Allen in the presence of the Lord Mayor, the Vice-Chancellor of the University of Liverpool, and Sir Thomas Beecham who conducted the opening concert. At last, the phœnix had risen from the ashes.

Herbert Rowse, the architect, described the Hall as being 'shaped like a megaphone with the Orchestra at the narrow end,' while Whittington-Egan's verse from 'Liverpool Roundabout' runs -
    'On Saturday night the town hums,
      but it is in a windowless shell
      suspended in space that the music
      of Liverpool sounds.'
Later on, the same author comments '... the atmosphere within that shell is most definitely timeless for, entirely without windows, it excludes the external world of day and night'.

The Fire (1933)

The second Philharmonic Hall floodlit (1957)

The interior of the Hall showing the Proscenium in position for use.

View of the auditoriim from the platform

Once again, Liverpool had produced a building both excellent for sound and agreeable to the eye, besides being a good deal more comfortable than the old auditorium. In design the Hall 'is similar to a 'thirties cinema, and music and architecture, two corresponding arts have been brought together in the building. The idea of composition in brick and stone as "frozen music" has become an actual physical fact'.

The Hall received its musical baptism when Sir Thomas Beecham conducted the first of three concerts to celebrate the opening. The programme was calculated to test the acoustics from every possible angle, including the great organ, an instrument totally enclosed in chambers situated behind the grilles flanking the sides of the Orchestra. The Console is placed on a lift-floor which can be lowered below stage-level when the organ is not required. When on stage-level the Console can be turned in any direction so that the organist can face the conductor and have the keyboard facing the audience.

Another feature, the Hall's cinema equipment, is unique in this country. The screen, together with the loud speaker and proscenium are all carried on an electrically-controlled rising and falling stage-lift. This lift weighs seven tons and when it is in position below stage the top of the proscenium becomes part of the floor of the platform.

The new Hall, when opened, was greatly admired by other Music Societies for its up-to-the-moment facilities especially that of the Orchestra being able to rehearse, audition and record in its own home, something no other British orchestra could do. At that time, changing rooms and space for instruments were adequate and everything appeared set for the resumption of a great tradition. Plans for the centenary celebrations in 1940 were being made, but before the season could start the country was plunged into the Second World War so that the jubilant plans for the 1939-40 season had to be abandoned. Disruptions were caused by a ban on evening concerts, evacuation, the departure of younger men for various forms of war work and the difficulties experienced by Manchester members in travelling between their city and Liverpool. For a century the Hallé and Liverpool Orchestras had members in common.

During the war the Society survived by combining with Louis Cohen's Merseyside Symphony Orchestra, and actually flourished as many London players moved to the North West. A valuable wartime schedule of weekly Subscription Concerts was held on Tuesdays while Sunday afternoon programmes contained popular music. Inevitably, the 1940 centenary year of the Society had to be celebrated quietly, and a special concert conducted by Hamilton Harty contained no unusual features beyond an historical note in the programme by A.K. Holland and a facsimile of the first 1840 concert programme.

Though Liverpool suffered severely from air raids in 1940 and 1941, the Luftwaffe was unable to bring the Phil to its knees. In fact, the almost miraculous survival of the new Hall amid terrible devastation, seemed to symbolise the indomitable persistence of æsthetic and spiritual values. Audiences flocked to experience a couple of hours' respite from the horrors and frustrations surrounding them, and were augmented by men and women of H.M. Forces temporarily resident in Liverpool, foreign soldiers, sailors and airmen,and emigrés. It was at this time that the 'scientific' purpose for which the Hall was originally dedicated, came into its own. The developments in cinematography had been such that the Hall's fine cinema equipment enabled the building to double as a cinema. With Rowse's screen rising out of the platform, the enjoyment of watching films at the Phil became an essential part of life in wartime Liverpool.

The opening of the new Hall and the ravages of war brought about rapid changes in the outlook of the Society, and soon it became apparent that nothing less than a permanent Orchestra would satisfy the musical requirements of the City. While this was a welcome development, it brought with it financial worries and in 1942 the Society entered into an agreement with the Liverpool Corporation whereby the latter acquired the Hall but agreed to pay an annuity. Free use of the Hall was given to the Society provided that a stipulated number of concerts was promoted and a permanent Orchestra maintained. Unfortunately, a stormy relationship between Corporation and Society was to develop in the future and not be resolved until the late 'eighties.

In 1942, the Orchestra was a full-time hard-working body giving some sixty Liverpool concerts (spread over three series) plus many out-of-town performances, broadcasts, schools' concerts and recordings. The practice of sharing players with other orchestras ended and the Liverpool Philharmonic's national standing was at a height when, with the recently-appointed Principal Conductor, Dr. Malcolm Sargent, it made its first London appearance in 1944, at the Royal Albert Hall Promenade Concerts. At this time, it was the best known provincial Orchestra in the country, through its popular recordings on His Master's Voice and Columbia.

The Brave New (post-war) World was one of enormous changes that were reflected at the Phil. The policy of selling seats permanently, with members displaying their names on brass plates on boxes, had gone up in flames with the old Hall. Without forgetting its most loyal patrons, the Society began to build a new audience through the Philharmonic Club and the Industrial Concerts, both of which started in 1946. The former organised monthly lectures on music, attracting a new and interested group of member-supporters which continues today as the Friends of the Phil, an organisation which contains loyal and active patrons. Under inspired and sensitive leadership, this group has developed today into one which faithfully upholds the Society, supports the Orchestra during foreign tours and raises needed money in a variety of ways. The

Industrials were conceived to enable the new, post-war workforce to enjoy classical music at a democratic, single low price. These proved to be so successful that in 1948-49 the series of eight programmes had to be given in quadruplicate.

In 1948, Hugo Rignold took over the conductorship and, despite protests about his suspiciously Jazz background, was eventually judged a success. Under his baton, members of the Orchestra played at the Festival of Britain in 1951 and the loyal Philharmonic Club chartered a train to London to support them.

It was during the 1940s that the Phil's ghost was first seen. The authority for this is Walter Runacus, forty-three years on the Phil's staff and the person to whom this booklet is dedicated. Walter's mother had been housekeeper to the general manager at the time of the re-building of the current Hall in the 1930s. In charge of cleaning, she was probably the first person to see the white lady who haunts the corridor behind the boxes to the right of the auditorium on the Caledonia Street side. Walter's mother, one morning, was told by a perturbed cleaner that she was unable to clean one of the boxes because a lady was sitting there. "Well, go in and ask her if she would mind moving", replied Mrs Runacus but the cleaner was reluctant. On entering the box, Mrs Runacus was just about to speak when the lady looked up and said, "Your son is not dead; he is safe". Walter's elder brother was serving in Crete at the time and notification had reached the family that the whole of his regiment had been wiped out and that he was presumed dead. Naturally, she was so amazed that she quickly turned round, forgetting the purpose for which she was in the box, and left for the corridor. Suddenly, remembering the lady, she turned to find her gone and not by the usual exits. Later that week, official Home Office information confirmed what the ghostly lady had said. Mrs Runacus's son was a prisoner-of-war but he was safe and well and later came home.

The white lady has been seen by a few people since, including the Hall's former electrician and always on the Caledonia Street side where the foundations of the previous Philharmonic Hall, burned down in the 'thirties, are the only part of the old building to remain.

The Philharmonic Society had taken a long time to re-build the second Hall, but A. K. Holland in an article in 'The Liverpolitan' commented that the Society 'has faced the future with some courage, and that it will possibly pull through.' Whether it did or not is to be revealed in Section III.

iii
Home of a 'Royal' Musical Centre

Towards the end of A. K. Holland's section are the words, 'I am afraid I can see no sign so far that it (the Society) intends to make any radical change in its policy. The new hall, despite its modern equipment, is designed to preserve the old atmosphere of social distinction, and the concerts, at prices which must be inevitably charged if the standard of the concerts is to be maintained, will be mainly the preserve of those who can afford them. The promised "Democratisation" of the most important musical society in Liverpool will not come off'. Holland goes on to make the valid point that the new Hall's capacity is smaller than that of the old one therefore prices must be high. To him, the most serious question is 'whether musical enterprise which has, in the interregnum, adapted itself elsewhere, will once more be led back to the musical centre which we all trust the new Philharmonic Hall will become'. Whether people were led back to 'the musical centre' or not will be assessed prior to the close of this section.

With the end of the war 'the goings on' in the Hall developed and expanded with the passing of each decade despite severe difficulties and problems at first. The dispersal of many orchestral players from Liverpool back to London as well as the generally unsettled conditions in the country, raised innumerable problems, particularly financial. Public subsidy on a large scale to professional artistic ventures such as orchestras was something quite new in Great Britain and there was literally a day-to-day struggle against impending bankruptcy. Fortunately, courageous and farsighted people guided the Society through these troubled days and under the Resident Conductor, Hugo Rignold, the Orchestra developed a reputation for adventurousness in its repertoire. It was during this period that firm foundations for the future were laid in a most extensive system of concerts for schoolchildren with the Liverpool Education Authority and also other Authorities on Merseyside and in Lancashire. The Industrial Concerts previously mentioned, provided another aspect of musical experience for industrial and office workers.

The Liverpool record of appointing young men to important posts was followed in 1957 when John Pritchard at the age of thirty-five was selected to be Musical Director and Conductor. He quickly proved that the Society's choice was fully justified. Under his direction a number of exciting, new musical ventures and a parallel development of the Orchestra's quality and style brought the work of the Society into national prominence.

The most important venture was a series called 'Musica Viva' in which four concerts each season, introduced by the conductor from the podium, were devoted exclusively to new and experimental music. A great deal of rehearsal time was given to these works which would have been quite impossible without the free use of the Hall.

The Society's success during the post-war period was rewarded in 1957 when both it and the Orchestra were granted royal patronage. Thus encouraged, another experiment, proving very successful, was the institution of an annual International Competition, one for conductors in 1958 and one for pianists in 1959. The first winner of the International Competition for conductors was Zubin Mehta, one of today's leading conductors. Held at two-yearly intervals, succeeding competitions were won by Dietfried Bernet in 1962 who had a highly successful career; Moshe Atzmon in 1964, an acclaimed Israeli conductor born in Hungary, and Johann van der Merwe in 1966 who was a South African. The interest aroused by all these ventures led to the Orchestra being engaged for six programmes at the London Promenade Concerts in August 1960, and for two concerts at the Edinburgh Festival the same year.

The fourteen years that Sir Charles Groves held the Music Director's post (1963-77) were years when the Royal Liverpool Philharmonic Orchestra demonstrated its quality further and more widely than ever before, both on disc and in performance. With Sir Charles Groves the RLPO became the first British orchestra to perform all the Mahler symphonies, and out-of-town appearances became more regular. This built a loyal following for the 'Liverpool Phil' in many other cities and towns. Over fifty concerts each year were given outside Liverpool including three successful subscription series in Blackburn, Preston and Warrington. Lunchtime recitals were, and continue to be, given while the Rodewald Concert Society now sadly disbanded, promoted a series of Chamber Concerts. The now 'Royal' Liverpool Philharmonic Choir founded in 1840 played an essential role in the Society's concerts as it still continues to do.

The Orchestra's first tour abroad took place in 1966 with a visit to Germany and Switzerland. Since then, it and the Choir, have been regularly in demand as an international touring combination. It was during the early 'seventies that Liverpool became the only professional music society in the country to run an Orchestra, Choir and Youth Orchestra. The Society took over the Merseyside Youth Orchestra in 1972 and professional players continue to give tuition to the young amateurs as they did in the past.

The period between the 'fifties and the close of the 'seventies was one of progress and stability in spite of financial and other problems. Fortunately, as in most areas of life there were the lighter moments. One such happened during the 'seventies when members of the League of Welldoers were attending an entertainment at the Hall and the stage had to be made smooth for a performance by seals. For some reason the performing seals were transported to the Hall by taxi which drew up at the main entrance instead of the side artistes' entrance. You can imagine the surprise of Walter Runacus and other staff members when they saw the seals slip out of the taxi, slide into the main Hall entrance and calmly make their way up the stairs!

Walter also remembers the day of John Pritchard's removal from London to Liverpool where he, like Sir Charles Groves, lived privately in the area. He had an open sports car and a crowd gathered round to see the cats and caged birds which had made the long journey in the back of the car.

There were the awkward moments when the lights failed and a concert was in progress; when the Von Trapp Family did not have the proper papers and it took over half an hour before they could go on stage, and the occasion when a Menuhin concert was sold out but severe fog prevented people from attending. Only sixty people managed to reach the Hall that evening.

On another occasion the guest of honour at a Society concert of music and a reception was the late Mr. Harold Wilson, and Walter was to look after the security men. A girl asked Walter if he could possibly obtain the Prime Minister's autograph for her. He asked, but the reply was "Not now - see you later." After the concert, a surprised Walter was told by a breathless security man, "The Prime Minister is looking for you!" Almost immediately, Mr. Wilson suddenly appeared and quickly gave his autograph. By this time the girl had given up hope and gone, so Walter has the autograph in his programme to this day.

The audiences during the thirty years so briefly covered were good for all the concerts in the Hall and elsewhere, and particularly for the Industrials where the same reduced price was charged for any seat in the Hall, including boxes. How amazed would those people of the previous hundred years be could they see who was sitting in their expensive and privileged seats. This change alone indicates that 'democratisation' had taken place since the war years. People from all social classes could attend, as they can now, and book tickets for any part of the Hall.

By 1980, the Hall had certainly become a fine 'musical centre' and at the end of Sir Charles Groves's tenure in 1977, there followed a decade in which three conductors held the Principal post, each for three years - Walter Weller, David Atherton and Marek Janowski. Since the mid-'eighties, Professor Ian Tracey has been Chorusmaster of the (Royal) Liverpool Philharmonic Choir which has achieved success in its own right through its recordings and foreign tours.

For a short period in 1986, it seemed as if a disaster as great as the 1933 fire was looming. Merseyside County Council was abolished and the possibility of the Philharmonic Hall being closed down and sold off was very close. Eventually, and with the help and support of its members, the Society signed a lease for the Hall in March, 1988. From then onwards, it has opened its doors as a resource that will benefit the whole community. Over the years, people have certainly been led back to the 'musical centre' which benefits everyone and not just the privileged.

During the past, but to a greater extent in the 'eighties', the Society has forged ever-widening links with London; with many other British cities such as Edinburgh, York, Bristol, and with a number of towns covering an area from Carlisle in the north to Leicester (East Midlands), Wells, Bath and Poole on the south coast. International tours have been numerous, but the links with Liverpool and Merseyside (to illustrate which has been one of the main objectives of this booklet) have extended rapidly. From being an organisation just providing regular concerts in a Hall, the work of the Society has grown over the years to include music for schoolchildren; individual and group teaching by members of the Orchestra; playing in such venues as the Arena Theatre of the International Garden Festival; in works' canteens; for the Granada TV spectacular 'New Brighton Rock'; for employees of the Vauxhall and Ford Plants at Halewood; in both of Liverpool's Cathedrals; floating on a stage in the Albert Dock for Granada TV; accompanying films and working with two thousand Liverpool schoolchildren when they made a recording of 'The Valley and the Hill', originally commissioned by Liverpool Education Authority for the Queen's Silver Jubilee visit to Merseyside.

It was during a later visit to the Hall by the Queen and at the time of the Falklands War that Walter Runacus will never forget. He had to keep an alert eye on all the security arrangements so he felt rather annoyed when interrupted by what he considered a joking telephone call. "This is Buckingham Palace" announced a voice. "Stop messing about" was his reply. "Could you contact the Queen's equerry immediately," continued the voice. The 'Sheffield' had been sunk and the Queen in the Phil's royal box, number twenty-two, had to be told the tragic news at once. Even when listening to a concert, Her Majesty must constantly be aware of the affairs of the community and the world outside.

The expansion of links with the local community has been one of the Society's main objectives during the present decade and reference will be made to this in the final section. Meanwhile, the Interlude introduces two conductors for whom Liverpool was to become a city of friendship and affection.

iv
Interlude: A Symphony of Friendship

Though John Pritchard had an apartment in the city he did not really know Liverpool as intimately as Sir Charles Groves who lived in Aigburth during his period of conductorship. His early life had been spent in London and the photograph on page 24 taken about 1927 shows him as the smiling goal-keeper (in pullover) of St Paul's Cathedral Choristers' football team. It was in London, also, that his musical career began, and in 1945 he was invited as a guest conductor to Liverpool. This was a foreshadowing of the golden years to come for himself and Lady Groves, and for the Orchestra. Sir Charles was appointed Music Director of the RLPO in 1963 and he and his family spent fourteen happy years settled in Fulwood Park where his beautiful home overlooked the River Mersey. The photograph on page 25 shows him in the music room with Zadok the marmalade cat looking out over part of the garden. True to form, like all genuine cat-lovers, Sir Charles was his slave and would always give up his chair if Zadok chose to settle there.

It was difficult at first for Sir Charles and Lady Groves to understand the Scouse accent, but eventually, they recognised an increasing number of words and came, over the years, to love Liverpool and its people. So, too, do their three children, though none was born here, but they are glad of any opportunity to visit the city. The grandchildren too, enjoy coming to Liverpool and especially Tom, who, at the age of two or three years, loved the ferry-boat crossing over the Mersey. If his grandparents stayed on the boat for several crossings as Merseysiders do, Tom thought that he was sailing to America!

Sir Charles was particularly interested in his work with young people and he and Lady Groves are seen on page 52 with members of the Merseyside Youth Orchestra. He quickly came to know the schools of Merseyside, whether they had choirs and of what quality, so that he could draw upon them if necessary. He also encouraged the visits to his home in Fulwood Park of a young, curly-haired boy who would stand entranced in the music-room looking at the rows of scores. He once remarked that he would love to own a similar number of scores himself one day. He grew up to become Sir Simon Rattle.

Sir Charles was a very democratic man and showed genuine interest in all that went on in the city. He would walk in Liverpool, especially in the 'docks'area; he had a really deep love of both cathedrals and always wore the tie of the Anglican Cathedral in which he and his family worshipped; he would certainly have appreciated the recent 1994-95 season of Philharmonic Concerts in the Anglican Cathedral which was used for performances while the Hall was being refurbished; he enjoyed visiting the

Walker Art Gallery and was a member of the Athenæum; during his time in Liverpool he was given an honorary degree by the University and by the then Polytechnic. He was particularly impressed by a plaque at that time in the greenroom of the Philharmonic Hall which told of a promise. This was (and is so to this day) that every local political party of any shade of opinion in power in Liverpool, promised to support the Society.

Sir Charles was present at the opening of the Metropolitan Cathedral, and he took the Orchestra out-of-town on occasions so that its achievements could become known to a wider public. Two occasions out of many are those at Leeds and London. During the Leeds Piano Competition one year, John Drummond made an excellent film for television which publicised the quality of the R.L.P.O. In Liverpool Anglican Cathedral Mahler's Eighth Symphony was performed in 1964 for the first time in the city. This performance was taken to the London Promenade Concerts which had that night the largest audience ever known at that time. This was only the third performance of the work in England and received a fifteen minutes' ovation.

Before moving into their Liverpool home, Sir Charles and Lady Groves stayed at the Adelphi Hotel. It happened to be Grand National Day. Unfortunately for them, by mistake and in all the excitement, their newly-brought luggage was taken back to London! All turned out well in the end, and they continued to stay until their home was ready. From the Adelphi, taxi-drivers would take Sir Charles, like his predecessors, to the 'Philly' - the taxi-men's name for the Hall.

"One important part of our lives," says Lady Groves, "was The Bluecoat Society and The Liverpool Mozart Orchestra of which Charles was President." Members of the Mozart Orchestra "played in our house each year to raise funds". Sir Charles was also President of the M.Y.O.

Both Sir Charles and Lady Groves had a special affection for the Preston 'Friends of the Phil' who, with Lady Grenfell-Baines and the Guildhall audiences, gave tremendous support to the Liverpool-based Orchestra. This past support (and present) linked with that of members of Merseyside's 'Friends of the Phil' is one of the Society's strongest assets.

Not only did Sir Charles Groves love Liverpool but he won the hearts of a big Liverpool public. Evidence of this affection was shown at his memorial service in the Anglican Cathedral where members of the M.Y.O. played, and in the tribute given on disc and tape by the Society. To the writer, one of the most touching tributes was one she was privileged to see. Sir Charles loved to wear ties and particularly those of the Anglican Cathedral and the Friends of the Phil. He left a hundred and fifty ties all of which have been cut and stitched into a large and beautiful collage which fills the whole of one wall of Lady Groves' London home. A gifted Preston lady, Josephine Ratcliff, lovingly and patiently completed this unusual and moving tribute.

The present Music Director, Libor Pešek, does not live in the city for his home is in Prague, yet he probably knows the area better than many Liverpudlians. During a television interview in 1990 the cameras followed him down the back streets of Liverpool. He was not content to be shown only the attractive parts of the city - he wanted to see the whole of 'the pool of life' of cosmopolitan Liverpool. Similarly, when he has the opportunity he enjoys visiting the city's bookshops or fruit barrows as much to meet the people as to see the books or fruit. Libor, as he likes to be called, wishes to be integrated with all the aspects of Liverpool life, not just the musical one. He once remarked, "I look upon the people of Liverpool as my 'family'." Proof of his sincerity in this statement is shown when he spoke of the tragedy of the Hillsborough football disaster where many Liverpudlians died. Libor expressed his sorrow and said that he felt the same sadness for them as he would if this had happened to Prague people.

Our conductor has seen a fair amount of the suburbs and surrounding areas, too. This has come about chiefly through invitations by Friends of the Phil for him to go on his 'free' evenings and be interviewed in different venues. Many of these have occurred over the years in such places as a private school in Hoylake, in South Liverpool, Burton and Ness Gardens in South Wirral, and in the Williamson Art Gallery, Birkenhead. One of the more unusual settings was at Martin Mere near Ormskirk. The room was surrounded outside by water containing tame and friendly birds. Libor, obviously interested, went outside to see them, but it is doubtful whether he had previously experienced the squawking of ducks during pauses in the talk!

In the city, he has officially visited the Liverpool Tate Gallery, the Athenaeum, the late Lyceum Club, the Departments of Music and Continuing Education of the University of Liverpool, the Walker Art Gallery and many other institutions, but perhaps one of the most unusual visit was to Lime Street Station. This happened on the 21st March 1990 when Jean Boht (Mrs Boswell from the TV series 'Bread') and Libor officially unveiled a nameplate entitled 'The Liverpool Phil' on an Inter-City locomotive. The 100 mph locomotive was named in honour of the Society's 150th anniversary, and members of the Society, Orchestra and Choir with Jean Boht and Libor as guests of Inter-City, travelled on the train to London. Despite being delayed for one and a quarter hours owing to signal failure, everybody arrived at the Barbican for the very successful 150th Anniversary Gala Concert.

It seems that the Czechs and the British share a similar sense of humour and find amusement in the same jokes and ridiculous situations. It gave Libor with his keen sense of humour, much delight to take part unexpectedly, with a few members of the Orchestra, in a play produced at the Playhouse. Dead bodies were required for a particular scene so Libor and the others happily obliged and became corpses!

Perhaps his feeling for the people of Liverpool and their problems is best illustrated by an article written by a previous Chief Executive of the Society in which he refers to a post-concert dinner held in Liverpool. In an improvised after-dinner speech Libor described his life as always having a background of decay and destruction. He had seen the destruction of Czechoslovakia as one of Europe's great democracies in 1938; the destruction of the Nazis and the further destruction of his country in the late 'forties and 'fifties. When he came to Liverpool for the first time in 1986 he saw a city in decay, but since then and "for the first time in my life, decay is being transmuted by a dynamic regeneration". This personal statement about Liverpool encourages all lovers of our city, and institutions like the Royal Liverpool Philharmonic Society are playing a vital part in this 'resurgence'.

Both the late Sir Charles Groves and Libor Pešek have set examples and encouraged the people of Merseyside to take a pride in their Orchestra and in their city. Thankfully, this pride is emerging as the twenty-first century approaches and reconstruction and renewal is taking place all over Liverpool. As part of this awakening a first-class home for the Orchestra has emerged in 1995 through the refurbishment of the present Hall.

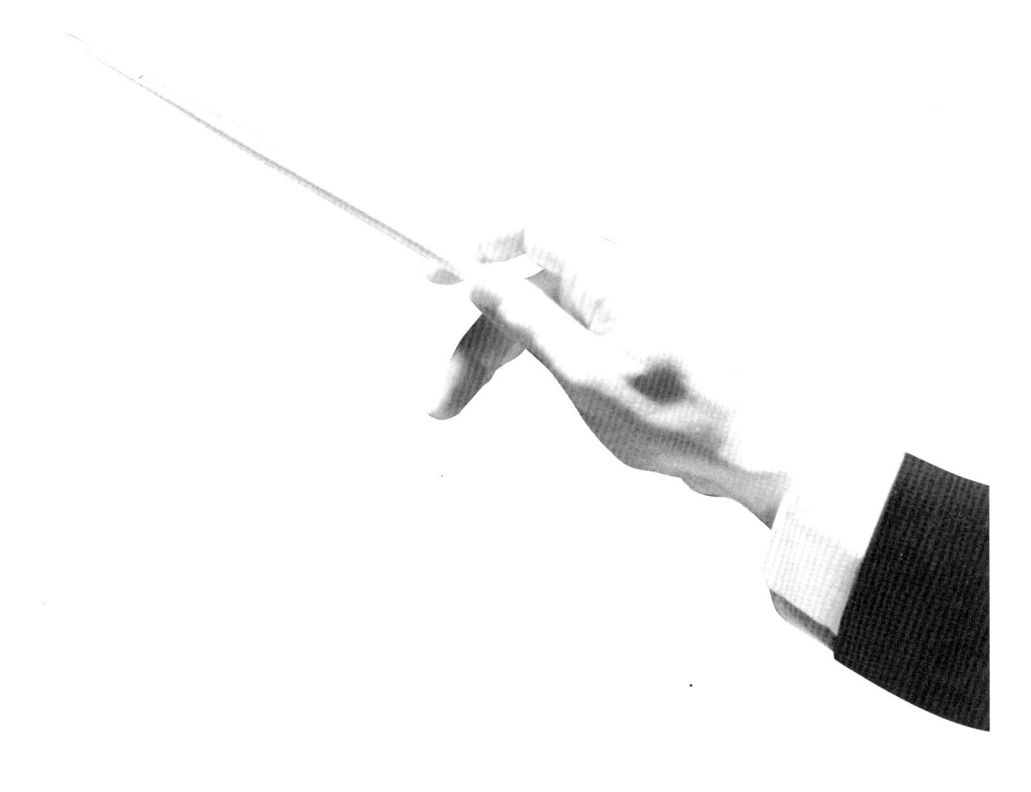

Group photograph taken on the occasion of Stephen Gray's Retirement Concert. Back row: (left to right) Simon Rattle, Walter Weller, Brian Pidgeon (general manager) Marek Janowski, David Atherton. Front row: (left to right) Sir Charles Groves, Stephen Gray, Libor Pešek

Sir Charles at leisure

Libor at leisure

St. Paul's Cathedral Choristers' Football team. Can you spot the young Charles Groves? Answer is in the text of the previous chapter.

Libor and Jean Boht at Lime Street Station

Sir Charles, with Zadok, at home in Fulwood Park

A thoughtful Libor at the Albert Dock

A First-Class Home for a World-Class Orchestra

After a period of fifty-five years of constant use, including many Sundays, the present Hall was found to be in much need of refurbishment. The structure cannot be altered because it is a grade two listed building, but it became essential that such important work as re-wiring, replacing or re-covering seats, enlarging the platform and balcony, and fitting a new, but similar,carpet, was carried out. Additionally, work was undertaken to improve the acoustics. Many older people felt that the acoustics, so excellent in their day, did not need improvement especially as the Hall's acoustical conditions were originally equal to those of the finest concert halls in the world. Since those days, technical knowledge of acoustics has advanced considerably, so a fine opportunity has occurred to take advantage of bringing the acoustical design up-to-date.

Other renovations included extending front-of-house facilities for patrons by creating new spaces for an open-plan Box Office and Phil Shop area. This work was the first to be completed and was used by patrons attending the 1993-4 season of concerts. Similarly, a new extension known as the Peter Moores Wing, attached to the Hall and containing the Rodewald function suite, administrative offices and better facilities for members of the Orchestra have been in use for some time.

Further improvements can be seen in the provision of new and better catering areas, bars, cloakrooms and washing facilities. A new control-room has emerged and air-conditioning, heating, lighting and ventilation has improved owing to technological advances. The exterior of the Hall has been renovated and cleaned, with ramps provided for wheelchair-users. The ramps are protected by a low wall of bricks which have been cleverly made to tone in with the original bricks used in the late 'thirties.

This refurbishment of the Hall has been crucial to achieving the degree of service to customers, sponsors and other users of the building, which the Society feels they deserve, and the Hall belongs to the Society - an unique asset. The development is responsible for broader benefits to the community of Merseyside.

The completed building looks most attractive both externally and internally, yet the purpose of a building, however attractive, is for the use of people. Great and varied use is made of the Hall by the Society which has an administration of thirty-nine full-time employees. It employs the Royal Liverpool Philharmonic Orchestra of eighty-three musicians giving one hundred and forty concerts each season, of which eighty are promoted at the Hall, the Society's home and the Orchestra's main venue.

R.L.P.O. Musicians at the Albert Dock

Philharmonic Hall with 150th Anniversary Flags

R.L.P.O. and R.L.P.C. performing Mahler 8 at Liverpool Anglican Cathedral

The Library of the Athenæum

The late Lyceum Dining Room

Athenæum Dining Room

Entrance to the Athenæum

Tate Gallery Liverpool, Albert Dock

Martin Mere

Paul McCartney during rehearsal in the Anglican Cathedral for his Oratorio

The rector of the then Polytechnic, Professor Peter Toyne (black and gold robes) with Wing Commander Sir Kenneth Stoddart and Libor on his left, and Professor Ian Tracey on his right.

Centre for Continuing Education, University of Liverpool

Liverpool Playhouse

Not everybody realises that a wide variety of music including jazz and ethnic music takes place at the Hall to complement the main programme of classical music.

As a venue for general entertainment, lectures, meetings, graduation ceremonies and school speech days the Hall serves as an ideal building. Now re-opened, and with greatly improved facilities, many different groups of people are being encouraged to use the building on those days and evenings when there are no R.L.P.O. rehearsals and concerts. Since it was opened in 1993 the spacious Rodewald Suite is always available to the public for private hire so there is the possibility of enjoying weddings, parties or other celebrations there.

The pleasant and varied lunch-time concerts return to the Hall's auditorium. During the 'away from home' season these have been held in the Everyman Theatre. These concerts last for approximately one hour and it is possible to take a meal either before or after the performance. Similarly, at the other end of the day, the occasional pre-concert talks given in the Rodewald Suite provide interesting and illuminating information about some of the music one is going to hear.

Children and young people are catered for, too, with Schools' Concerts given by the Orchestra in the Hall and supported by the Liverpool Education Committee and the four Local Authorities of Wirral, Sefton, Knowsley and St Helens. Outside Merseyside, Lancashire and Cheshire Local Authorities are also supportive.

Younger children enjoy special Saturday morning concerts which are open to all children. The programmes called 'Sounds Alive' are varied, lively and exciting and usually attract a good audience.

Information about all these events is to be found at the Hall's Box Office. (See page 39)

Throughout its history, the Society and its Orchestra have made a national and international mark on the musical world, and so it is fitting that a world-class Orchestra has a first-class home from which to embark upon its exciting future.

A section of the Orchestra at the end of a concert

vi
Coda: Into the Future with the Hall's Ambassadors from Liverpool

All that was mentioned in Section V takes place when the Orchestra returns to its attractive restored 'home' during the Autumn of 1995. This is the basis of the Society's work with its world-class Orchestra, but the writer sees two important aspects of the work which are likely to develop in the future. These are an increase in foreign tours, provided financial support is available, and a rapid advance in building upon the work already achieved in taking the 'Phil' and all for which it stands, into the community.

As early as February, 1992, the Orchestra made its first tour of the United States of America. Sponsored by the Merseyside Development Corporation the Orchestra played in eleven venues including Washington, Boston and New York. This was the first time that any orchestra had acted as an 'ambassador' for its region and this it did most successfully. The object was to promote important cultural and economic links with the U.S.A. The combined efforts of the Merseyside Development Corporation and the Orchestra attracted much interest in the Merseyside region and successful business links were promoted.

Despite the problem of the Hall's closure for refurbishment the Orchestra's 1994 schedule included three foreign tours - to Asia, Germany and Austria, and to Spain. These tours are costly in terms of money, planning, organisation and time but all of them benefit Liverpool and Merseyside. How can this be so when the majority of local people probably do not know about these tours? Members of the Society and Orchestra, Choir and M.Y.O. are all Merseyside's ambassadors when they perform anywhere (including Britain) outside Liverpool. They give an impression of what Merseyside is like and can achieve, and the high standard of performance arouses both admiration and interest. As a consequence further invitations are made, tourists visit our city and area, and business houses consider the possibility of trade. Every Merseysider benefits indirectly as a result.

Just as these foreign tours are responsible for these benefits so the work of the Society in contacting the local community has similar results. In 1988 the Community Education, Publications and Special Projects Department was established, at that time the only one connected with a Symphony orchestra in this country, and which had a full year of activities from 1989 to 1990.

New Grand Foyer

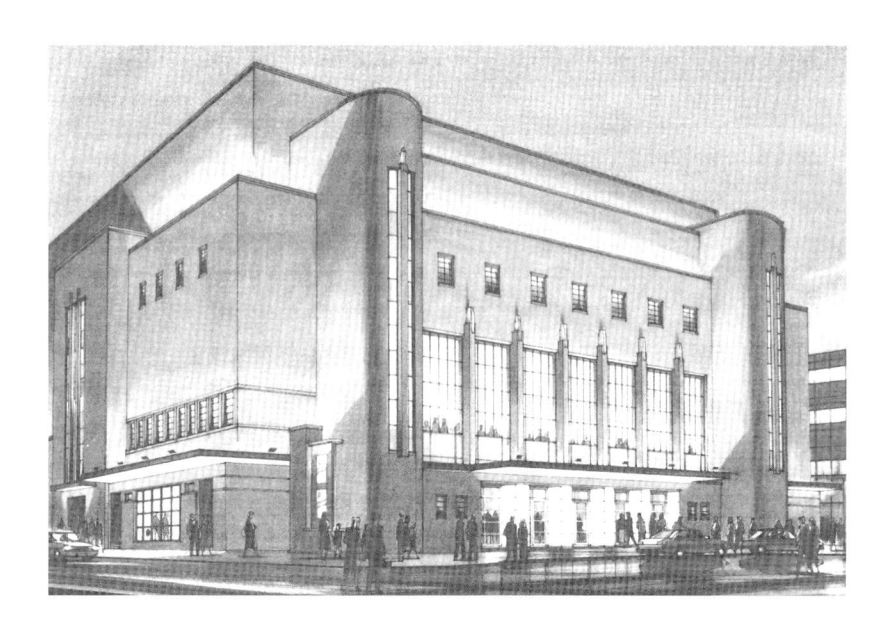

Exterior of the Refurbished Hall

Antony Lewis-Crosby
the present Chief Executive

The present Chairman
Brian Thaxter

Both are totally committed to the Society and work devotedly for its well-being and for that of the transformed phoenix

The pleasure of a full house!

During that year contact was made through projects with two 'special needs' schools in St. Helens; work was carried out in two Liverpool 8 primary schools through collaboration with the Education Department of the Tate Gallery, Liverpool; a project centred on women living on the New Street Estate in St. Helens explored 'Women's Lives' through drama and music workshops which proved to be the most developmental undertaken during the year; the Department collaborated with the Performance and Communications Skills post-graduate course of the Guildhall School of Music for an intensive week-long project in the Cheshire Borough of Halton; work was carried out with young offenders in an open prison; a GCSE music composition course was carried out in two Wirral Secondary Schools, and the year's work finished with a project at All Saints High School, Kirkby concerned with composition involving three ensembles from the school. This list reflects the wide variety of work in the community being carried out by the Society through its special Department for that purpose.

Since that first year similar and more extensive contacts have been made with the elderly, ethnic groups, and the handicapped. The policy of the Society is to take music in a variety of forms to those who are unable to visit the Hall. These people gradually begin to realise that all that 'goes on in the Hall' is as much for them as it is for concert-goers. It is worth speculating again upon how amazed would the box- and stalls-holders of the last century be if they could witness this democratic change of policy! Though the majority of people enjoying these projects are never likely to visit the Philharmonic Hall, some of the children do and certainly enjoy the visit.

Benefit from this work in the community is not one-sided. Sections and individual members of the Orchestra taking part have their experiences broadened and their sensitivity sharpened by the contacts made. This meeting with a variety of people is the very best way of showing that the music of the Royal Liverpool Philharmonic Orchestra and Choir is not just for the chosen few; it is for the enjoyment of all who find pleasure in music. Similarly, the refurbished Hall has its doors open to every member of the community.

Everybody connected with the Hall from the cleaners, technicians, administrative staff, Orchestral, Choir, M.Y.O. members, and Board of Management works for the good of the Society and supports the world-class Orchestra and Choir which are so much appreciated by people abroad and in the rest of Britain. As owners of the Philharmonic Hall, the Society is in an unique position in this country in providing a permanent home for the Orchestra, Choir, and Youth Orchestra in which they can rehearse, perform, and record, so giving them a major artistic advantage. The success of any artistic organisation relies upon a chemistry for excellence - an unique coming-together of circumstances, personalities and ideas, which can set standards for a community and provide a vision of what that community embodies. Such an unique chemistry exists in the relationship between the Orchestra and its Music Director, Libor Pešek, who has extended his contract and will be with the Society for the foreseeable future. The Society and its members look forward to a long association with him, with the hard-working, dedicated Chief Executive, and with the Orchestra and Choir.

Once returned to its refurbished home, the Society's ambition in future years is to position the Orchestra as pre-eminent among the country's regional orchestras and competitive internationally with the London orchestras through its foreign tours and recordings. Most importantly, the Society will continue to serve the Merseyside region with the highest possible standards of music-making and provide an environment at the Philharmonic Hall suited to those standards yet warmly reflective of the democratic attitude towards all people who enter its doors.

Whether we have associations with the Hall or not, we are all presently living during a vital and important period of its history which now covers a period of a hundred and forty-six years. The extensive and fascinating material held in the archives so patiently preserved, sorted and treasured with love and devotion by Mr. Vin Tyndall is open to inspection by all who have a genuine interest.

Why not come and see the 'new-look' Hall for yourself? It is possible that you may have enjoyed the lighter orchestral music provided during the 'Summer Pops' season in the Big Top near the Albert Dock. If so, then you can hear some similar music included in other programmes, particularly The Classic Series, or at Christmas. Unlike conditions up to forty years ago, the Hall welcomes everybody. It is your Hall and has much to offer for your enjoyment and for that of every member of your family. You will be pleasantly surprised.

Every person in the Society contacted in connection with the publication of the booklet has been most approachable and helpful. Sandra Parr, Betty Green and Ian Archer are representative of them all.

Some Useful Information

The Philharmonic Hall is open for visitors just to call in and look around without the obligation of buying tickets. Your questions will be answered and there are leaflets available to take home. For those anxious to attend concerts the following information is for quick reference.

1 Where to Book
Call in at the Box Office at the Philharmonic Hall, open from 10.00 am to 5.30 pm Monday to Saturday, and 10.00 am to 7.30 pm on concert nights.

You can book by telephone using Access or Visa on 0151-709-3789.

2 Eligibility for Discount
Students, under-l8s, disabled and unwaged can buy single tickets (in advance) at 25% discount from the Philharmonic Hall Box Office on production of the appropriate identity.

3 Save with a Standby
On concert days only, if you are a senior citizen, student, under-18, disabled or unwaged you can purchase any remaining tickets from the Box Office at half-price on production of the appropriate identity.

4 Disabled Patrons
Special ramps give entrance to stalls and boxes with adjacent wheelchair spaces which can also be used for guidedogs. Tickets (including subscription tickets) for patrons in wheelchairs and those who are partially sighted are available at half-price.

5 Group Booking Discount
Saturday Series and Wednesday Series, 15% off ticket prices for groups of 10-49 in numbers and 20% off for all groups of 50 or over is offered. Additionally, 2 complimentary tickets are given with all orders of 50 tickets and over.

6 Youthcard
If you are under 18 you qualify for membership of our Youthcard Scheme. Call in to the Box Office with a passport photo and proof of your age to obtain your Youthcard for £2.50 and you'll be able to purchase single tickets for all concerts in our Saturday and Wednesday Series at 50% discount.

7 How to join the Friends of the Phil (Membership of the Society)

You can join for one year, four years or for life. If two people are resident at the same address you can take advantage of our joint rate and if you are under 24 you qualify for our Young Person's rate. The benefits are as follows:-

(a) Priority booking for all R.L.P.O. and R.L.P.C concerts including the Christmas Carol Concerts.
(b) Bi-monthly mailings with 'Encore' Newsletter, advance details of forthcoming events and special offers.
(c) Special discounts at Lunchtime Concerts.
(d) Free passes to open rehearsals.
(e) Exciting day trips to R.L.P.O. concerts and prestigious musical events around the country.
(f) Opportunities to join the R.L.P.O. on foreign tours.
(g) Free membership of your Friends of the Phil 'Local Group' for more social and musical events in your area.
(h) Voting rights as a Member of the Society and eligibility for election to the R.L.P.S. Board of Management.

Application leaflets with the various rates can be obtained from the Philharmonic Hall or by post to the following address:

> Box Office ('Friends of the Phil'),
> Philharmonic Hall,
> Hope Street,
> LIVERPOOL
> L1 9BP

If you require any further information just call 0151 709 3787.

A group of 'Friends' in St.Stephen's Square, Vienna (1994)

OPENING AUTUMN SEASON 1995

The all new .....
Philharmonic Hall Liverpool

One of the country's most distinguished concert halls will now become one of the country's most sought after music and entertainment centres as the magnificent 1,700 seat Philharmonic Hall re-opens in September 1995 following its major £9 million refurbishment.

Philharmonic Hall

Libor Pesek Music Director RLPO

As always . . .
home to the world class Royal Liverpool Philharmonic Orchestra . . .

As always . . .
an art deco masterpiece and one of the most handsome concert halls in existence . . .

Now with . . .
a wide ranging international music and entertainment programme including resident and visiting orchestras, solo recitals, touring shows, pop, jazz, folk, film, comedy, cabaret . . .

New Grand Foyer Bar

Now with . . .
an aggresive marketing and sales package including full promotional literature, direct mail, distribution, advertising, media support . . .

Now with . . .
entirely reorganised technical facilities including 2,750 sq ft stage space, full production lighting and sound (including Dolby Cinema), full tour rigging capability, technical crews and backup . . .

The only art deco full suite cinema screen in the world

1995-96 Classic Film Season

Now with . . .
even more impressive acoustics . . .

Now with . . .
all new seating, foyers, bars, bistro, catering, function, conference and reception suites . . .

Full range of deals available. For more information and bookings contact the Philharmonic Hall Director, Andrew Bentley, on 0151 709 2895 (phone), 0151 709 0918 (fax).
Philharmonic Hall, Hope Street, Liverpool L1 9BP

Wine & dine in style

Make your evening complete with a delicious meal before the concert in the new hall's magnificent basement restaurant in the new Manweb Suite. Appetising starters, mouthwatering main courses and delicious sweets will be available as well as a wide choice of beverages in our Grand Foyer and Balcony Bars. And why not order your interval drinks before going in to the concert to save time later?

For special occasions you can book the Rodewald Suite with expert catering specially tailored to your personal requirements. For further information telephone our Events Co-ordinator on 0151–709 2895.

Late night shopping!

Why not take away a memento of your evening at the Philharmonic Hall? The Phil Shop is open throughout the evening with a full selection of RLPO recordings, memorabilia as well as a wide range of musical and other gifts for all ages.

Our Service to you

Philharmonic Hall is blessed with an enthusiastic and knowledgeable team of highly trained front of house staff whose task is to make every minute of your evening enjoyable. Comments should be directed on the night to the duty House Manager or in writing to the Philharmonic Hall Director, Philharmonic Hall, Hope Street, Liverpool L1 9BP

Park your car with confidence

BCP – Oldham Street Car Park

Parking in the streets around Philharmonic Hall is limited so we recommend the use of Oldham Street Car Park, just a five minute walk from the Phil. This fully staffed and secure facility is open on concert nights from 5.30pm until midnight so you can enjoy your evening out in complete confidence. Parking with BCP costs only £1 per evening when pre–booked through the RLPS. To reserve your parking space just complete the booking form on page 25 and we will send you your parking vouchers with your concert tickets.

Euro Car Park – Caledonia Street

The Caledonia Street Car Park situated next to Philharmonic Hall is available during concert nights and a fee will be levied on arrival. This facility is limited and is not available for pre–booking.

Public Transport

Merseytravel's SMART buses, numbers 3 & 4 run every fifteen minutes every day of the week. This service links Hope Street with the City Centre, Lime Street and Central Station. Further information is available from the Merseytravel line on 0151–236 7676.

R.L.P.O. Principal Conductors

•1840•
John Russell Thomas Clough William Sudlow
•1844•
Zeugheer Herrmann
•1865•
Alfred Mellon
•1867•
Julius Benedict
•1880•
Max Bruch
•1883•
Sir Charles Hallé
•1895•
Sir Frederick Cowen
•1913•
Sir Henry Wood Sir Thomas Beecham and Guest Conductors
•1942•
Sir Malcolm Sargent
•1948•
Hugo Rignold
•1955•
Efrem Kurtz
John Pritchard
•1963•
Sir Charles Groves
•1977•
Walter Weller
•1980•
David Atherton
•1983•
Marek Janowski
•1987•
Libor Pešek

Max Bruch

Sir Charles Hallé

Sir Frederick Cowen

Sir Henry Wood

Sir Thomas Beecham

Sir Adrian Boult

Dr. J E Wallace

Louis Cohen

Sir Malcolm Sargent

Hugo Rignold

Herbert Rowse

John Pritchard

Walter Weller

Vernon Handley

Geoffrey Cowie

Edward Warren

Chorusmasters of the R.L.P.C.

Though it can claim to be slightly older, the Liverpool Philharmonic Choir came into being officially at the same time as the Orchestra, when the Society was founded in 1840. From its first concert during that year which consisted of glees, rounds and madrigals interspersed with instrumental items, the Society has maintained and developed its strong and varied choral tradition. Choral singing is so much a part of the Society's tradition that there was once a time when if the Choir was not singing and 'new-fangled' symphonies were introduced, the audience, particularly the die-hards in it, would open newspapers 'which were not folded again until the choir was about to give voice ...' (The Liverpolitan, 1934).

For the first forty years the Chorus, as it was then known, was usually directed by orchestral conductors such as William Sudlow from 1840 and Zeugheer Herrmann who became director in 1844. Visiting conductors, too, would direct the Chorus which, in those days, took part in every performance. It was not until 1844 that the symphony appeared in the programme and caused the strong reaction by certain members of the audience to which reference is made in the previous paragraph.

In the mid-1840s the Chorus of one hundred voices and called 'practical members' played a leading part not only in the programme but in the administration, even setting up its own Auxiliary Committee which seems to have made its own decisions and carried them out, often without even consulting the parent body! The members also carried out amicable warfare with Zeugheer Herrmann, usually over the matter of tempo. This was to come to a head at the first performance of 'Elijah' in the new Hall in 1849 and 1850, when serious disagreement over the pace of the Baal choruses nearly caused disaster.'The Philharmonic chorus-singer had his notions of what was right and proper, and meant to show Herrmann that to beat one instead of three in a part of the Baal scene was a thing not to be tolerated' (Argent,1889).

The twelve year conductorship of Julius Benedict from 1867 to 1879 had been both beneficial and profitable to the Society, 'and may be said to have established the definitive form of its concerts which was to prevail for the next fifty years' (Taylor, 1976). He was succeeded by Max Bruch 'who insisted on assuming the threefold office of conductor, chorusmaster and pianoforte accompanist ...'.

It was not until 1883, upon the appointment of Charles Hallé as director, that the Philharmonic Committee appointed an official Chorusmaster -Horatio Arthur Branscombe who remained for over forty years with thirty of these as Chorusmaster.

Choral music predominated in the Society's programmes during and just after World War I because of the scarcity of orchestral musicians.

With the establishment of a full-time professional Orchestra, the Choir became an integral part of the main concert series in the Philharmonic Hall, and, as now, was heard in broadcasts on B.B.C. Radio 3 and on recordings.

Two long-serving Chorusmasters were Dr. A. W. Pollitt 'that fine musician and rare spirit' (The Liverpolitan, 1934), and Dr. J. E. Wallace OBE, both of whom are still remembered with great affection and respect by older Merseyside people. Dr. Wallace was born and educated in Liverpool, gave distinguished musical service as lecturer in Music in the University, and to the Matthay School of Music; had been organist at Ullet Road Church from the time he was eighteen; was music master at Liverpool Institute, Liverpool Collegiate, Blackburne House, and Queen Mary High School, and served the Society for forty years.

Dr. Wallace enjoyed teaching children and it was he who established the well-known Liverpool Christmas Carol Concerts. These were developed by his successor, Edmund Walters, Chorusmaster for fifteen years. He built upon the work of Dr. Wallace and was a composer. He contributed much to Liverpool through his work with the Society's annual Carol Concerts, and by his position as Head of Music to the I.M. Marsh Teachers' Training College and Music Director of the University's 'Gilbert and Sullivan' Society.

The present Chorusmaster, Professor Ian Tracey, succeeded in 1985, and he has travelled with the Choir both nationally and internationally. As well as performing in many of the major concert venues in the North-West and the Midlands, the Choir has appeared frequently at the Royal Albert Hall Promenade Concerts, sung regularly with the B.B.C. Philharmonic, and made successful appearances in France and Spain. With the Orchestra, in 1992, the Choir was invited to tour Spain and gave six performances of Mahler's 'Symphony of a Thousand', a performance of Paul McCartney's 'Liverpool Oratorio' at the Olympic Stadium in Barcelona, and two concerts at Expo '92 in Seville. During the summer of the same year, they sang in 'Fanfare for a New World', an opera gala televised nationally from Liverpool's King's Dock.

The R.L.P.C. has recorded Vaughan Williams's 'A Sea Symphony', 'Sinfonia Antarctica' and 'Serenade to Music', also Herbert Howell's 'Hymnus Paradisi' and 'An English Mass' with Vernon Handley, and Finzi's 'Intimations of Immortality' with Richard Hickox. Other recordings include Borodin's 'Polovtsian Dances' and Beethoven's 'Ninth Symphony' with Sir Charles Mackerras, Paul McCartney's 'Liverpool Oratorio' with Carl Davis and Suk's 'The Ripening' with Libor Pešek. Their recording of 'Flos Campi' with the R.L.P.O. and Vernon Handley won the 1988 BPI Best Classical Record Award. Their latest releases include Elgar's 'Dream of Gerontius' under Vernon Handley with the R.L.P.O. and the Huddersfield Choral Society and 'Carols from Liverpool' with the Philharmonic Brass under Ian Tracey.

It is owing to the dedication, skill and musical ability of the present Chorusmaster that the R.L.P.C. has reached such a high standard of achievement.

CHORUSMASTERS APPOINTED BY THE PHILHARMONIC COMMITTEE

1883	Horatio Arthur Branscombe
1913	Harry Evans (Resident Choral Conductor)
1914	R H Wilson
1917	Alfred Benton
1918	Dr. Arthur W. Pollitt
1929	Dr. J. E. Wallace
1970	Edmund Walters
1985	Ian Tracey (now Professor)

Professor Ian Tracey

The Merseyside Youth Orchestra

'The inspired thought which created the M.Y.O. was the joint idea of Alderman David Lewis and William Jenkins who became conductor for over 21 years' (Kenneth Stern, Director of the Society, on the occasion of the 25th Anniversary Concert, 22nd May, 1976). The message continued, 'I must emphasise how fortunate we are to have the advice and help of an international conductor of the reputation of Sir Charles Groves. He has always taken a great interest in the M.Y.O. ...'.

From the foundation of the Youth Orchestra in 1951, Geoffrey Cowie played in the first violins. 'He has maintained a very close and active connection with the orchestra, ever since becoming Deputy Conductor in 1963' (Kenneth Stern, 25th Anniversary Concert), and since the early 'eighties has been Chairman of the M.Y.O.

Up to 1972, the Youth Orchestra was administered by a Committee consisting of representatives of the Society and of Education Authority officials. Since then, the Society has taken full responsibility for the Orchestra which has its own Music Director and a supportive group of people, mainly parents, who form the Friends of the MYO. The Orchestra has developed into one of the finest Youth Orchestras in the country and its successes have been numerous. For example, in 1979 a Selection Committee chose the M.Y.O. to play in the National Festival of Music for Youth at the Fairfield Halls, Croydon. In the same year they were selected to play in the Schools' Prom in the Albert Hall, London. This was repeated in 1982.

In the early 'seventies Simon Rattle assisted William Jenkins with rehearsing the M.Y.O. especially when they attended the fourth International Festival of Youth Orchestras in Lausanne, Switzerland. Since then they have undertaken the following tours:-

1975	Belfast Festival. France
1978	Berlin
1980	Israel
1983	Aberdeen International Youth Festival
1989	Czechoslovakia/Germany
1991	Brittany
1993	Austria/Germany
1995	Holland/Belgium

Organisation and arrangements for all the M.Y.O.'s concerts and foreign tours have been undertaken by the indefatigable and experienced Sandra Parr, Orchestra Director.

Sir Charles and Lady Groves with M.Y.O. members during a presentation by Ken Stern on behalf of the Youth Orchestra (1976)

Members of the M.Y.O. during a concert (1984)

LIST OF PHOTOGRAPHS

Photographs are listed in order of appearance and are reproduced by courtesy of the institutions or individuals named in brackets.

1	Sir Desmond Pitcher (R.L.P.S.) page	i
2	Walter Runacus (John Mills Photography Ltd.)	ii
3	The Concert Hall (R.L.P.S.)	v
4	The Philharmonic Hall and New Chapel (R.L.P.S.)	3
5	Exterior of New Philharmonic Hall at Liverpool (R.L.P.S.)	3
6	Evening Concert at the Philharmonic Hall (R.L.P.S.)	4
7	A Damaged Plaque and Picture of Clara Butt (R.L.P.S.)	7
8	The Fire (1933) (R.L.P.S.)	9
9	The second Philharmonic Hall floodlit (1957) (R.L.P.S.)	9
10	The interior of the Hall showing the Proscenium in position for use (R.L.P.S.)	10
11	View of the auditorium from the platform (R.L.P.S.)	10
12	Picture of a conductor's hand (R.L.P.S.)	21
13	Group photograph taken on the occasion of Stephen Gray's Retirement Concert (John Mills Photography Ltd.)	22
14	Sir Charles at leisure (Lady Groves)	23
15	Libor at leisure (R.L.P.S.)	23
16	St.Paul's Cathedral Choristers' Football Team (Lady Groves)	24
17	Libor and Jean Boht at Lime Street Station (Liverpool Daily Post and Echo, plc.)	24
18	Sir Charles, with Zadok, at home in Fulwood Park (Lady Groves)	25
19	A thoughtful Libor at the Albert Dock (R.L.P.S.)	25
20	R.L.P.O. Musicians at the Albert Dock (R.L.P.S.)	27
21	Philharmonic Hall with 150th Anniversary Flags (R.L.P.S.)	27
22	R.L.P.O. and R.L.P.C. performing Mahler 8 at Liverpool Anglican Cathedral (R.L.P.S.)	28
23	The Library at the Athenaeum (John Mills Photography Ltd,)	28
24	The late Lyceum Dining Room (Fraser Communications)	29
25	The Athenaeum Dining Room (John Mills Photography Ltd.)	29
26	The Entrance to the Athenaeum	29
27	Tate Gallery Liverpool, Albert Dock (David Clarke)	30
28	Martin Mere (The Wildfowl and Wetlands Trust, Slimbridge)	30
29	Paul McCartney during rehearsal in the Anglican Cathedral for his Oratorio (R.L.P.S.)	31
30	Group with the rector of the one-time Polytechnic (Gerry Wood)	31
31	Centre for Continuing Education, University of Liverpool (Centre for Continuing Education, University of Liverpool)	32
32	Liverpool Playhouse (Liverpool Daily Post and Echo, plc.)	32
33	A section of the Orchestra at the end of a Concert (R.L.P.S.)	33

34 New Grand Foyer (Brock Carmichael Associates)	35
35 Exterior of the Refurbished Hall (Brock Carmichael Associates)	35
36 Antony Lewis-Crosby, present Chief Executive (R.L.P.S.)	36
37 Brian Thaxter present Chariman	36
38 The pleasure of a full house!	36
39 Sandra Parr, Betty Green and Ian Archer (Betty Green)	38
40 A group of 'Friends' in St.Stephens Square, Vienna (Joan McLarnon)	40
41 Max Bruch, Sir Charles Hallé, Sir Frederick Cowen, Sir Henry Wood (R.L.P.S.)	44
42 Sir Thomas Beecham, Sir Adrian Boult, Dr. J.E.Wallace, Louis Cohen (R.L.P.S.)	45
43 Sir Malcolm Sargent, Hugo Rignold, Herbert Rowse, John Pritchard (R.L.P.S.)	46
44 Walter Weller, Vernon Handley, Geoffrey Cowie, Edward Warren, (R.L.P.S.)	47
45 Professor Ian Tracey (R.L.P.S.)	50
46 Sir Charles Groves and Lady Groves with M.Y.O. members (Lady Groves)	52
47 Members of the M.Y.O. during a concert (1984) (R.L.P.S.)	52

References

1. The Times, 28th August, 1849
2. The Times, 30th August, 1849
3. The Times, 31st August, 1849
4. Liverpool Philharmonic Society Annual Report for 1852
5. Liverpool Review, 12th January, 1889, V.XX, no.1048, (pp4-5)
6. The Liverpolitan, December, 1934, V.III, no.12, (p14)
7. General information and background knowledge from ARGENT, W.I.(1889), The Philharmonic Jubilee: Half-a-Century of Music in Liverpool, Egerton Smith and Co. Reprinted from the 'Liverpool Mercury'.
8. BENAS, B.B.(1944) 'Merseyside Orchestras: An introduction to the history of local instrumental music', in Transactions of the Historic Society of Lancashire and Cheshire, v.95, Liverpool: printed for the Society.
9. HOLLAND, A.K. (1939), 'The new Philharmonic Hall', in The Liverpolitan, June, 1939 (p20).
10. STAINTON de B.TAYLOR (1974), Two Centuries of Music in Liverpool, Liverpool: Rockliff Brothers, Ltd.
11. WHITTINGTON-EGAN, R. (1976), Liverpool Roundabout, Manchester: E.J.Morten (pp71-72)
12. WRIGHT, S. (1990), A History, published by the Society for the 150th Anniversary.
13. All quotations taken from R.L.P.S. programmes, newsletters and other publications, and from radio and television interviews.